Number Plates

Story by Beverley Randell
Illustrations by Sarah Davis

William was ten years old.
He could read his own name
and write it, too.
He could read his sister's name,
Charlotte,
and his mother's name,
Jane,
and his father's name,
Mark.
And William could read books
to his teacher at school.

William

Best of all, William liked reading number plates. When they were out in the car, he would play a number plate game with Charlotte, who was six.

They tried to find a number plate for each letter of the alphabet.

William took a photo of each number plate with his tablet.

"There's an *A*!" William would shout.

"And there's a *B*," Charlotte would say.

Then it would be William's turn to find a *C*.

One Sunday morning,
all the family went swimming.
William was a good swimmer,
and he swam all the way
down to the end of the pool
and back again.

On the way home,
William and Charlotte
played the number plate game.
They had just seen a *D* and an *E* and an *F*,
when Dad stopped outside the supermarket.

"We need some bread and milk," said Dad.
"Does anyone want to come with me?"

Charlotte got out of the car.

“I don’t want to come,” said William.
“I swam all that long way. I’m tired.”

“You can stay in the car with me, then,” said Mum.

William looked out the window for a number plate with a *G* on it.

Then, William saw a white car
come into the car park.
It was going very fast,
and it went round and round
the car park without stopping.
The driver made his wheels spin.

Bang!

The white car bumped into the back of William's car, and then it raced out of the car park.

When Dad and Charlotte came out of the supermarket, they were just in time to see the white car racing away.

They ran over to see if Mum and William had been hurt.

"We are all right," said Mum,
"but look at our broken light!"

"Did you see the number plate?" said Dad.

"No!" said Mum. "I'm sorry.
They were going too fast."

GMT 58

"I did," said William.
"I got their number.
Look! Here it is.
GMT 588."

"You got their *number*!" shouted Dad.
"Well done, William!
Now we can tell the police
the number plate of the car
that hit us."

"That was clever, William,"
said Charlotte.

“And I found a *G*, too,”
said William.
“I’m good at reading number plates.”